Writing Sparks

Prompting Conation

PEARSON
SkyLight

Glenview, Illinois

Writing Sparks: Prompting Conation

Published by Pearson Professional Development
1900 E. Lake Ave., Glenview, IL 60025
800-348-4474 or 847-657-7450
Fax 847-486-3183
info @ skylightedu.com
http://www.skylightedu.com

ISBN 1-57517-917-2

V

ZYXWVUTSRQPONMLKJIHGFEDCBA
10 09 08 07 06 05 04   15 14 13 12 11 10 9 8 7 6 5 4 3 2

Contents

Introduction

Conation is a powerful concept that can have a very positive effect on students in today's schools. Conation is self-motivation, determination, and self-effort that leads to change.

Personal beliefs can greatly influence conation. If teachers help students believe they can succeed, odds are that they will. This is reflected in the idea that how one perceives reality is what forms future reality. This idea is encompassed in Figure Intro.1, The Conative Paradigm, which visually demonstrates how a person's paradigm influences his or her worldview.

The conative intelligence is the ability to strive to reach goals and to persist in working toward goals. When teachers can awaken this intelligence in both themselves and students, the results are very powerful. If teachers can help students recognize and tap into their inner motivation, any student can achieve learning success.

The intent of this book is to provide teachers with writing activities and prompts to be used with students to foster a spirit of conation in the classroom. Each activity encompasses

The Conative Paradigm

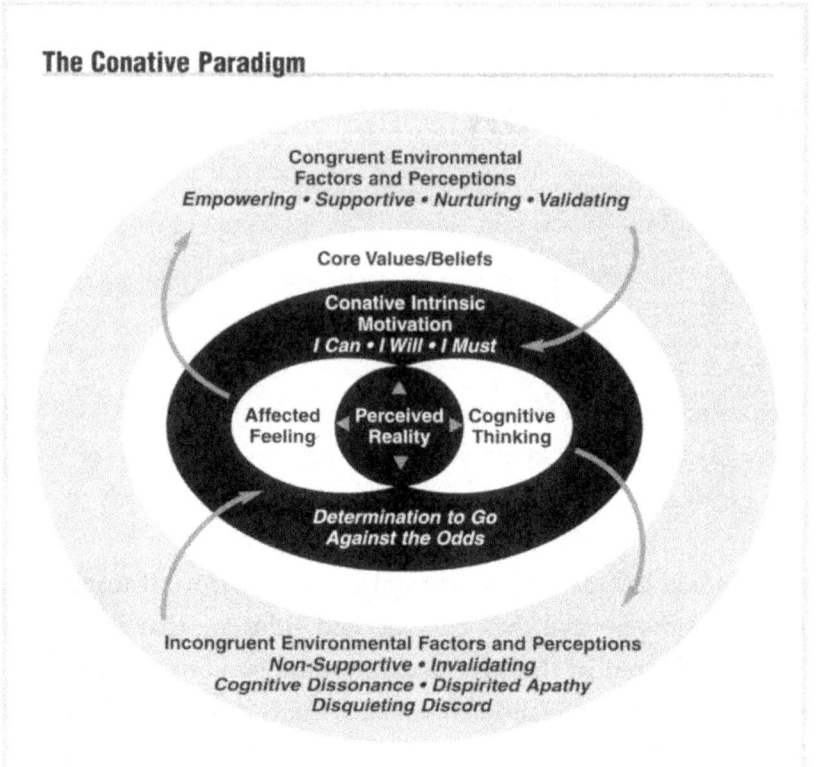

Congruent Environmental
Factors and Perceptions
Empowering • Supportive • Nurturing • Validating

Core Values/Beliefs

**Conative Intrinsic
Motivation**
I Can • I Will • I Must

Affected
Feeling

Perceived
Reality

Cognitive
Thinking

*Determination to Go
Against the Odds*

Incongruent Environmental Factors and Perceptions
*Non-Supportive • Invalidating
Cognitive Dissonance • Dispirited Apathy
Disquieting Discord*

Figure Intro.1

a characteristic of conation and encourages students to think about that tenet and how it can influence their lives. The writing activities can be effective with students of any age.

The writing activities that follow address the three main aspects of motivation that are cornerstones of conation: self-direction, self-observation, and self-reflection. These activities help focus students on moving forward, identifying ideas and goals, and developing plans for reaching those goals. They are meant to move students toward their goals, taking into account that when students write down their thoughts and goals they are more likely to achieve them.

There are nine writing activities encompassed in this book, plus one culminating activity that summarizes and builds upon the previous activities. Most of these activities can be completed in a class period, although the culminating activity may take a bit longer as it covers all three aspects of conation. There is also a section at the end of the book with some ideas to get teachers started in creating their own writing activities.

For each activity, space is provided for teachers to record notes and reflections on the activity and how the activity went when used in their classroom.

Self-Direction

S elf-direction is the desire and aptitude for setting goals and making plans. By becoming aware of values, thinking about possibilities for the future, and setting goals, students can move toward achieving success. Self-direction is an important component of conation because it allows students to focus on what is possible in the future, not just what is achievable right now. The following three writing activities focus on engaging students in self-direction.

Envisioning the Future

This activity helps students think about their plans for the future and visualize where they want to go. Envisioning the future offers students an opportunity to think about planning for future goals and what it would take to put those plans into action.

TO BEGIN THE ACTIVITY, ask students, "Where do you see your life 10 years from now?" Then, ask students to write a description of what they imagine their lives to be like.

To initiate thinking about this concept, offer the following questions as prompts:

- Conjure up an image of yourself in the future. Where are you? What are you doing?
- If your future could be anything, what would it be?
- What steps would it take to achieve your future?
- What values are important to have in your life? How might you incorporate these things into your life in the future?
- Do you have any role models or mentors who could help you along the way?

Notes

Reflections on the Activity

Setting Goals

This activity helps students set achievable goals for themselves in a measurable timeframe. Students can use these objectives to focus their attention on accomplishing more this school year.

TO BEGIN THE ACTIVITY, tell students "Set three goals for yourself that you would like to achieve by the end of the school year." Then ask students to describe the goals in detail in writing.

To initiate thinking about this concept, have a discussion prior to starting the writing assignment in which the class considers the following questions:

- What are goals?
- Is a goal something that is easy to achieve? Why or why not?
- Why are goals important?
- What different kinds of goals are there?

Notes

Reflections on the Activity

Achieving Goals

*This activity assists students in making plans for carrying out the
goals they wrote about in the previous activity. Making plans for
attaining ambitions is an important part of the conative process
because it provides students with a framework for making goals come
to life.*

To BEGIN THE ACTIVITY, ask students to think about the
goals they wrote about in the previous writing activity.
Be sure they have a copy of their goals to refer to. Tell students
"Write a plan for reaching each of the goals you wrote about.
Make sure to include solid steps for how you plan to achieve
each goal."

Have a discussion about goal planning to help students
better understand what goal planning looks like. One way to
get this conversation started is to ask questions such as the
following:

- Think of a goal you reached in the past. What were
  some of the steps you took to accomplish it?
- What kinds of characteristics are important to have in
  steps to meet a goal? (i.e., they should be practical, they
  should be consecutive, they should segue from one to
  the other)
- Why are steps useful when trying to meet a goal?

Notes

Reflections on the Activity

Self-Observation

Self-observation is an important skill for students to develop. By examining their thoughts and behaviors, students can learn more about themselves and the ways they choose to approach life experiences. Self-observation can also help students monitor energy they may be expending on negative thoughts or behaviors and work on replacing them with positive thoughts or behaviors. The following two writing activities focus on getting students thinking about self-observation.

Being a Problem-Solver

☼

This activity helps students pay attention to problem-solving skills so they understand strategies used to work out problems. They can then apply these strategies to tackle obstacles that stand in the way of their goals.

T O BEGIN THE ACTIVITY, tell students "Spend the following day recording any minor problems that crop up in your lives. Then write what steps you took to solve the problems."

To initiate thinking about the concept, hold a discussion prior to starting the writing assignment. Start by discussing the following questions with the class:

- What types of minor problems do you experience on a daily basis? (As a prompt, you may provide an example such as not being able to find homework, arguing with a sibling, etc.)
- How do you typically solve these problems?
- Does the way in which you solve problems usually work effectively?
- What are some good strategies for solving problems?
- Why is it important to think of ways to solve problems?

Notes

Reflections on the Activity

Negative/Positive

☼

This activity helps students replace negative, self-defeating thoughts with positive, confident thoughts. Students may not realize how often they criticize themselves until they sit quietly for a few minutes and let their thoughts bubble to the surface. Replacing negative thoughts with positive thoughts can help spur students forward and aid them in approaching their goals with confidence.

To BEGIN THE ACTIVITY, tell students "I'm going to start a timer for three minutes. I would like you to sit quietly, without speaking. During the three minutes, I want you to record any thoughts that might pop into your head. Write them down." When the three minutes are up, tell students "Take a look at the thoughts you have listed. For every negative thought you have listed, write a positive thought that reframes the negative thought. The goal of this activity is to get you to think about replacing your negative thoughts with positive ones."

To continue thinking about this concept, have a follow-up discussion with students after they complete the writing assignment. Ask the class the following questions to prompt discussion:

- What are some examples of negative thoughts?
- What are some examples of positive thoughts?
- How did you feel when you recorded your negative thoughts?
- How did you feel when you replaced your negative thoughts with positive ones?
- Why do you think it's powerful to replace your negative thoughts with positive ones?

Notes

Reflections on the Activity

Self-Reflection

Self-reflection is taking the time to think about one's thoughts and actions. Through self-reflection, students can focus on past actions to determine how their thoughts and actions have affected their lives, positively or negatively. By conducting this type of self-assessment, students can make more informed decisions and choices when they encounter similar situations in the future. The following four writing activities examine self-reflection.

Let's Get Motivated!

☼

This activity encourages students to reflect on what motivates them and think about how to steer their energy and goals toward those motivating factors.

To begin the activity, tell students "Think about the last time you were really motivated to do something. What was it? Why were you motivated?" Ask students to write about what it was that motivated them.

To initiate thinking about this concept, have a discussion prior to starting the writing assignment in which the class considers the following questions:

- How do you define motivation?
- What motivates you? Why?
- What can you do to motivate yourself?
- Why is it important to be motivated?
- How are motivation and achievement connected?

Notes

Reflections on the Activity

Future Thinking

☼

This writing activity helps students reflect on actions or experiences they've encountered in the past that they wish had gone differently, and to make plans for better handling a similar situation in the future. Being able to learn from mistakes is an important part of the conative process because it helps students analyze and adapt behaviors and actions to become more successful in school and in life.

TO BEGIN THE ACTIVITY, tell students "Think about the last time you did something you regretted. What was it? Write about how you might handle a situation like that one differently in the future, knowing what you know now."

To initiate thinking about the concept, have a discussion prior to starting the writing assignment. Ask students the following questions to get the conversation started:

- Why is it important to reflect on past experiences?
- How can thinking about something you would do differently if you had to do it over again help you in the future?
- How do your actions affect others?
- Do we have a choice in how we act?

Notes

Reflections on the Activity

Taking Risks

☼

This activity helps students think about risk-taking and when it can be useful in helping them get where they want to go. Calculated risk-taking is an important component of conation because it helps students to reach for the next level.

To begin this activity, tell students "Think about the last time you did something that took courage or involved taking a risk. Write about what you did and how you felt when you did it."

To initiate thinking about this concept, use the following discussion-starters before assigning the writing activity:

- How do you define risk-taking?
- When is risk-taking good, and when is it bad?
- What does it mean to take a calculated risk?
- What are some of the effects you've experienced from taking risks?

Notes

Reflections on the Activity

The Importance of Values

☼

This activity encourages students to begin thinking about what is important to them in order to define their values. Values are an integral part of mapping life goals.

To BEGIN THE ACTIVITY, tell students "Think about what in your life is most important to you. How does what is important relate to your values? Write a few paragraphs explaining the connection."

To initiate thinking about this concept, have a discussion prior to starting the writing assignment to foster thinking about values. Start by asking students the following questions:

- What are values?
- Are values important? Why or why not?
- What are some of your values?
- How do values link to goals?

Notes

Reflections on the Activity

Culmination

This activity combines and builds upon the three aspects of cona-tion—self-direction, self-observation, and self-reflection—that have been discussed in the previous writing activities. This activity involves aspects of previous activities so students can apply what they've learned to develop a comprehensive plan for achieving an objective that may otherwise seem unattainable.

T O BEGIN THE ACTIVITY, have students think about what they would most like to do if they could do anything at all. Ask them to open their minds and dream big—-thinking without limitations. Then explain that using what they learned from the self-direction activities, they are going to describe (in written form) what they would most like to do in their lives if there were no limitations.

Next, ask students to call on their self-observation skills by sitting quietly for a few moments and noticing what thoughts come into their heads when they picture themselves acting out their "dreams." Tell students to record their thoughts and how they feel…do they feel excited? scared? do any challenges or negative thoughts pop up that they might need to address before working to achieve their dreams? Ask them to write down the thoughts and feelings flowing through their minds.

Finally, ask students to use their self-reflection skills to develop a more formalized plan to reach their dreams. Ask them to look over what they wrote for their thoughts and feelings about achieving their dreams and reflect on what they can do to overcome challenges toward reaching them. Ask them what they might do to keep themselves moving forward when they feel frustrated. Then, ask them to spend a few minutes reflecting on and writing down the steps they would need to take to achieve their dream. Tell students to use as much detail as possible in describing their plans for achieving their ultimate goals.

To complete this activity, ask those students who are comfortable sharing what they've written to share with the class what their dream is and how they plan to achieve it.

Notes

Reflections on the Activity

Creating Your Own Writing Activities

You can aid your students in building their conative abilities by creating your own activities to use in addition to those provided in this book. To design activities that best fit the needs of your students, think about the motivational issues your students typically experience. The list below will help identify the areas in which your students might need more practice.

Do your students have trouble with...
(check all that apply)

1. __Setting goals for themselves
2. __Thinking about plans for the future
3. __Carrying out plans for the future
4. __Observing their behavior and correlating their behavior to outcomes
5. __Understanding what motivates them
6. __Knowing strategies to use to solve problems
7. __Motivating themselves to achieve a goal
8. __Understanding the importance of learning from past experiences
9. __Identifying their values
10. __Staying true to their values
11. __Being aware of their actions

If you have the most checks for numbers 1–3, you will want to focus your students on activities around self-direction. If you have the most checks for numbers 4–6, you will want to engage your students in activities related to self-observation. If you have the most checks for numbers 7–11, you will want to involve your students in activities around self-reflection.

If you have already completed the activities in this book that focus on these different areas and would like to extend your students' thinking in a certain area, review the following ideas to prompt thinking about additional activities. These activities can be used in group discussions, partner discussions, or be extended into individual writing opportunities. You can use these activities in their entirety, or simply as jumping off points for creating your own activities.

Self-Direction:

- Give each student an index card with the following words on it:

  - Who
  - What
  - When
  - Where
  - How

  Ask students to think about a goal they have for themselves and fill out the index card with how they intend to achieve the goal.

- Pair students up in groups. Ask them to conduct interviews with one another about their goals for the future. Let students know that the interviewees should detail steps for reaching their goals.

Self-Observation:

- Ask students to go through a day observing opportunities for showing caring or being empathetic towards another person. Ask them to write a description of the situation and how they reacted to it.

Self-Reflection:

- Read (or tell) your students a story with a character that engages in behavior that has consequences (good or bad). Hold a discussion with your students in which you ask them how the behavior influenced the consequences.

- Ask students to think about a movie, piece of music, book, or other type of art that motivates them. Ask them to write a description of the art and explain what about it motivates them, and why.

References

These resources provide more information on conation.

Ames, C. (1988). Achievement goals in the classroom: Students' learning strategies and motivation processes. *Journal of Educational Psychology, 80*(3), 260-267.

Barrell, J. (1995). *Critical issue: Working toward student self-direction and personal efficacy as educational goals.* Oak Brook, IL: North Central Regional Educational Laboratory.

Corno, L. (1992). Encouraging students to take responsibility for learning and performance. *Elementary School Journal, 93*(1), 69-83.

Gholar, C. R. & Riggs, E. G. (2004). *Connecting with students' will to succeed: The power of conation.* Glenview, IL: Pearson Professional Development.

Kiersey, D. (1998). *Please understand me II: Temperament, character, intelligence.* Del Mar, CA: Prometheus Books.

Maslow, A. (1954). Motivation and personality. New York: Harper.

Schunk, D. & Zimmerman, B. (Ed.) (1994). *Self-regulation of learning and performance: Issues and educational applications.* Hillsdale, NJ: Erlbaum.

Shapiro, L. (2003). *How to raise a child with a high EQ: A parent's guide to emotional intelligence.* NY: Quill.

www.ingramcontent.com/pod-product-compliance
Lightning Source LLC
Jackson TN
JSHW080038010226
97517JS00015B/165